Grammaropolis PRESENTS

THE MAYOR'S

VOCABULARY AND WRITING

JOURNAL

FUNKY WORDS FOR MIDDLE SCHOOLERS

BY ORDER OF

The Mayor of Grammaropolis

Written by Christopher Knight
Interior Design by Christopher Knight
Cover Design by Mckee Frazior
Grammaropolis Character Design by Powerhouse Animation & Mckee Frazior

ISBN: 9781644420492
Copyright © 2021 by Grammaropolis LLC
All rights reserved.
Published by Six Foot Press
Printed in the U.S.A.

Grammaropolis.com
SixFootPress.com

Grammaropolis PRESENTS

THE MAYOR'S

VOCABULARY AND WRITING

JOURNAL

FUNKY WORDS FOR
MIDDLE SCHOOLERS

GRAMMAROPOLIS BOOKS

HOUSTON

HOW TO USE THIS BOOK

PHONETIC PRONUNCIATION

SYLLABLE BREAKDOWN

DICTIONARY PRONUNCIATION

foofaraw

foo·fa·raw • [FOO-fuh-raw] • \ ˈfü-fə-ˌrȯ \

PART OF SPEECH

USAGE EXAMPLE IN A COMPLETE SENTENCE

- noun

DEFINITION

a great fuss or disturbance about something insignificant

My sister exploded into a massive **foofaraw** when I told her that someone had scratched her car, but I think she totally overreacted.

SYNONYMS

ANTONYMS

WRITE YOUR OWN SYNONYMS HERE

excitement

brouhaha

indifference

disinterest

WRITE YOUR OWN ANTONYMS HERE

WRITING TIME!

Use *foofaraw* in an original sentence of your own creation.

Last night at dinner my cat knocked over a glass of water and caused a real foofaraw.

PRACTICE USING THE WORD BY WRITING AN ORIGINAL SENTENCE

BONUS FUN TIME!

Express *foofaraw* with a drawing or invent a dictionary-style definition of your own.

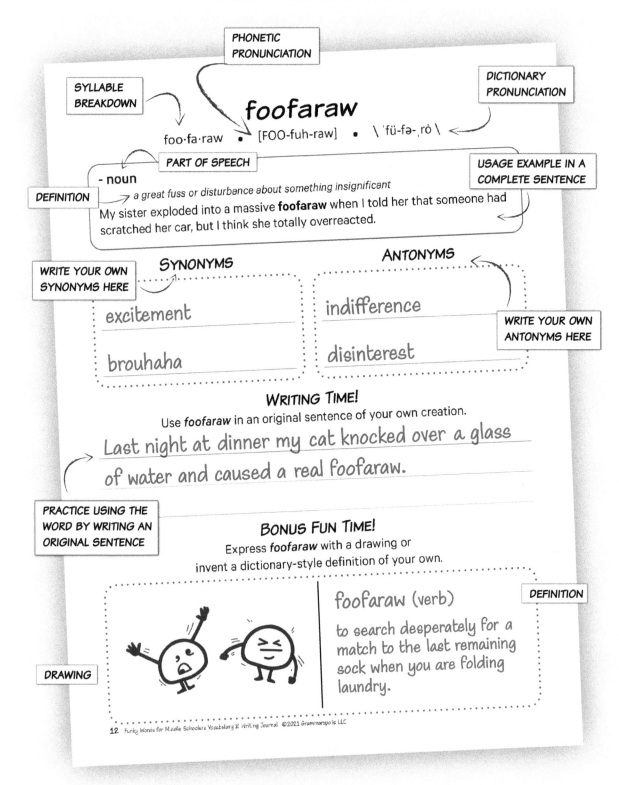

foofaraw (verb)

to search desperately for a match to the last remaining sock when you are folding laundry.

DEFINITION

DRAWING

TABLE OF CONTENTS

PARTS OF SPEECH REVIEW
Every word acts as at least one of the eight parts of speech.

In this workbook, you'll find nouns, verbs, adjectives, and one adverb. Here are some things you need to remember about them!

NOUNS
A noun can name a person, place, thing, or idea.

Naming a person:
Jason is my very best **friend**.

Naming a place:
Becks Prime is my favorite **restaurant**.

Naming a thing:
That **ball** is my favorite **toy**.

Naming an idea:
Honesty and **loyalty** are my best **qualities**.

VERBS
An action verb expresses mental or physical action, and a linking verb expresses a state of being.

Expressing physical action:
Richard **jumped** across the river.

Expressing mental action:
Richard **considered** jumping across the river.

Expressing a state of being:
Richard **feels** bad. He **is** sorry for jumping across the river.

ADJECTIVES
*An adjective modifies a noun or a pronoun and tells **what kind, which one, how much,** or **how many.***

Modifying a noun:
The **quick brown** fox jumped over the **enormous, new red** fence at the **first** sign of trouble.

Modifying a pronoun:
They are **satisfied** with the answer, but I am still **curious**.

ADVERBS
*An adverb modifies a verb, an adjective, or another adverb and tells **how, where, when,** or **to what extent.***

Modifying a verb:
Dayton **quickly** ran **home** so that he would arrive **early**.

Modifying an adjective:
Dayton was **extremely** tired after running.

Modifying another adverb:
Dayton ran **very** quickly.

There are four other parts of speech you won't find in this workbooks, but that doesn't mean they're not important! Here they are:

PRONOUNS
A pronoun takes the place of one or more nouns or pronouns.

PREPOSITIONS
A preposition shows a logical relationship or locates an object in time or space.

CONJUNCTIONS
A conjunction joins words or word groups.

INTERJECTIONS
An interjection expresses strong or mild emotion.

SECTION ONE: WORD PREVIEW
Welcome to your fourteen new favorite words!

When you encounter new words, it's a good idea to think about them for a bit. Lucky for you, here's a chance to do just that!

    1. Try to determine the part of speech. What part of speech does it *feel* like to you?

    2. Do your best to come up with a brief definition.

agroof
Part of Speech: n. v. adj. adv.

*Definition:*_____

_____

animadversion
Part of Speech: n. v. adj. adv.

*Definition:*_____

_____

cachinnate
Part of Speech: n. v. adj. adv.

*Definition:*_____

_____

clishmaclaver
Part of Speech: n. v. adj. adv.

*Definition:*_____

_____

foofaraw
Part of Speech: n. v. adj. adv.

*Definition:*_____

_____

fugacious
Part of Speech: n. v. adj. adv.

*Definition:*_____

_____

gesticulate
Part of Speech: n. v. adj. adv.

*Definition:*_____

_____

logorrhea
Part of Speech: n. v. adj. adv.

*Definition:*_____

_____

obfuscate
Part of Speech: n. v. adj. adv.

*Definition:*_____

_____

panegyric
Part of Speech: n. v. adj. adv.

*Definition:*_____

_____

rapscallion
Part of Speech: n. v. adj. adv.

*Definition:*_____

_____

refulgent
Part of Speech: n. v. adj. adv.

*Definition:*_____

_____

taradiddle
Part of Speech: n. v. adj. adv.

*Definition:*_____

_____

vouchsafe
Part of Speech: n. v. adj. adv.

*Definition:*_____

_____

agroof

a·groof • [ah-GROOF] • \ əˈgruːf \

> **- adverb**
>
> *in or into a prone position, face down*
>
> Susan tripped on the sprinkler and fell **agroof** right onto the ground.

SYNONYMS

ANTONYMS

WRITING TIME!

Use *agroof* in an original sentence of your own creation.

BONUS FUN TIME!

Express *agroof* with a drawing or
invent a dictionary-style definition of your own.

animadversion

an·i·mad·ver·sion • [an-uh-mad-VER-zhun] • \ ˌa-nə-ˌmad-ˈvər-zhən \

> **- noun**
>
> *a critical comment or comments, especially those reproaching somebody*
>
> Jaxon didn't think he'd done anything wrong, but his report card was filled with **animadversion** instead of praise.

SYNONYMS

ANTONYMS

WRITING TIME!

Use *animadversion* in an original sentence of your own creation.

BONUS FUN TIME!

Express *animadversion* with a drawing or
invent a dictionary-style definition of your own.

cachinnate

cach·in·nate • [KAK-uh-nayt] • \ ˈka-kə-ˌnāt \

- verb

to laugh loudly or immoderately

I couldn't enjoy the movie because the guy in front of me **cachinnated** the whole time.

SYNONYMS

ANTONYMS

WRITING TIME!
Use *cachinnate* in an original sentence of your own creation.

BONUS FUN TIME!
Express *cachinnate* with a drawing or
invent a dictionary-style definition of your own.

clishmaclaver

clish·ma·cla·ver   •   [KLISH-mah-klay-ver]   •   \ klēsh-məˈklāvər \

> **- noun**
>
> *casual chat or gossip*
>
> My friends and I were supposed to study last night, but we spent most of the time sharing **clishmaclaver** instead.

SYNONYMS

ANTONYMS

WRITING TIME!
Use *clishmaclaver* in an original sentence of your own creation.

BONUS FUN TIME!
Express *clishmaclaver* with a drawing or
invent a dictionary-style definition of your own.

foofaraw

foo·fa·raw • [FOO-fuh-raw] • \ ˈfü-fə-ˌrȯ \

- noun

a great fuss or disturbance about something insignificant

My sister exploded into a massive **foofaraw** when I told her that someone had scratched her car, but I think she totally overreacted.

SYNONYMS

ANTONYMS

WRITING TIME!
Use *foofaraw* in an original sentence of your own creation.

BONUS FUN TIME!
Express *foofaraw* with a drawing or
invent a dictionary-style definition of your own.

fugacious

fu·ga·cious • [fyoo-GAY-shuss] • \ fyü-ˈgā-shəs \

- adjective

  1. fleeting or passing away quickly
  2. lasting only briefly before withering or dropping

An unexpected goal gave the fans a **fugacious** hope that their team would win.

SYNONYMS

ANTONYMS

WRITING TIME!

Use *fugacious* in an original sentence of your own creation.

BONUS FUN TIME!

Express *fugacious* with a drawing or
invent a dictionary-style definition of your own.

gesticulate

ges·tic·u·late • [jes-TICK-yoo-late] • \ je-ˈsti-kyə-ˌlāt \

- verb

to gesture with the arms or hands especially when speaking

My teacher **gesticulates** so loudly during her lectures that it looks like she's drowning.

SYNONYMS

ANTONYMS

WRITING TIME!
Use *gesticulate* in an original sentence of your own creation.

BONUS FUN TIME!
Express *gesticulate* with a drawing or
invent a dictionary-style definition of your own.

logorrhea

log·or·rhe·a • [log-ah-REE-ah] • \ ˌlȯ-gə-ˈrē-ə \

- noun

excessive, incoherent talkativeness

Instead of being able to eat his dinner in peace and quiet, Franklin had to endure his cousin's **logorrhea** throughout the entire meal.

SYNONYMS

ANTONYMS

WRITING TIME!
Use *logorrhea* in an original sentence of your own creation.

BONUS FUN TIME!
Express *logorrhea* with a drawing or
invent a dictionary-style definition of your own.

obfuscate

ob·fus·cate • [ob-fyoo-SKATE] • \ ˈäb-fə-ˌskāt \

- verb

1. to make so confused or opaque as to be difficult to perceive or understand.
2. to render indistinct or dim; darken

I didn't exactly lie, but I definitely **obfuscated** enough so that my sister couldn't be sure that I'd eaten her pudding .

SYNONYMS

ANTONYMS

WRITING TIME!

Use *obfuscate* in an original sentence of your own creation.

BONUS FUN TIME!

Express *obfuscate* with a drawing or
invent a dictionary-style definition of your own.

panegyric

pan·e·gy·ric • [pan-uh-JEER-ick] • \ ˌpa-nə-ˈjī-rik \

> **- noun**
>
> *extravagant praise delivered in formal speech or writing*
>
> After the president's electrifying speech, newspaper columnists couldn't have been more effusive with their **panegyric**.

SYNONYMS

ANTONYMS

WRITING TIME!

Use *panegyric* in an original sentence of your own creation.

BONUS FUN TIME!

Express *panegyric* with a drawing or
invent a dictionary-style definition of your own.

rapscallion

rap·scal·lion • [rap-SKAL-yen] • \ rap-ˈskal-yən \

- noun

a rascal; a scamp

Always be alert around my cousin; he's such a devious **rapscallion**.

SYNONYMS

ANTONYMS

WRITING TIME!
Use *rapscallion* in an original sentence of your own creation.

BONUS FUN TIME!
Express *rapscallion* with a drawing or
invent a dictionary-style definition of your own.

refulgent

re·ful·gent • [rih-FUL-junt] • \ ri-ˈfŭl-jənt \

- adjective

shining brilliantly or splendidly

We were all impressed by your **refulgent** holiday decorations.

SYNONYMS

ANTONYMS

WRITING TIME!

Use *refulgent* in an original sentence of your own creation.

BONUS FUN TIME!

Express *refulgent* with a drawing or
invent a dictionary-style definition of your own.

taradiddle

tar·a·did·dle • [TAR-ah-did-el] • \ ˈta-rə-ˌdi-dᵊl \

- **noun**

    1. a petty falsehood; a fib
    2. silly pretentious speech or writing

Don't go around spouting **taradiddles** if you want to appear trustworthy.

SYNONYMS

ANTONYMS

WRITING TIME!
Use *taradiddle* in an original sentence of your own creation.

BONUS FUN TIME!
Express *taradiddle* with a drawing or
invent a dictionary-style definition of your own.

vouchsafe

vouch·safe • [vouch-SAFE] • \ vaúch-ˈsāf \

> **- verb**
>
>   *1. to undertake or deign to grant or give something*
>   *2. to promise, agree, or allow something (formal)*
>
> The famous chef **vouchsafed** his secret recipe to his only daughter.

SYNONYMS

ANTONYMS

WRITING TIME!
Use *vouchsafe* in an original sentence of your own creation.

BONUS FUN TIME!
Express *vouchsafe* with a drawing or
invent a dictionary-style definition of your own.

Section One: Word Review

Congratulations on learning fourteen more amazing words! Remember that the whole point of learning new vocabulary is to actually use it, so let's put your new vocabulary to use.

1. Review the words you've learned. Consider what comes to mind when you say the words themselves. How about when you read the definitions?
2. Circle at least **three** of your favorites. You'll get to use these in your very own story.

agroof ————— adverb

in or into a prone position, face down

animadversion ——— noun

a critical comment or comments, especially those reproaching somebody

cachinnate ——— verb

to laugh loudly or immoderately

clishmaclaver ——— noun

casual chat or gossip

foofaraw ——— noun

a great fuss or disturbance about something insignificant

fugacious ——— adjective

1. fleeting or passing away quickly;
2. lasting only briefly before withering or dropping

gesticulate ——— verb

to gesture with the arms or hands especially when speaking

logorrhea ——— noun

excessive, incoherent talkativeness

obfuscate ——— verb

1. to make so confused or opaque as to be difficult to perceive or understand.
2. to render indistinct or dim; darken

panegyric ——— noun

extravagant praise delivered in formal speech or writing

rapscallion ——— noun

a rascal; a scamp

refulgent ——— adjective

shining brilliantly or splendidly

taradiddle ——— noun

1. a petty falsehood; a fib
2. silly pretentious speech or writing

vouchsafe ——— verb

1. to undertake or deign to grant or give something
2. to promise, agree, or allow something (formal)

STORY ONE

1. List the words you've chosen:

_____

2. Write a story that incorporates all of your chosen words. If you can't think of anything to write about, consider these suggestions:
   - Write a story in a world where people can fly and it's no big deal.
   - Write a story in which your main character owns a chocolate factory.

Title:_____

_____

_____

_____

_____

_____

_____

_____

_____

_____

_____

Section Two: Word Preview
Welcome to your fourteen new favorite words!

When you encounter new words, it's a good idea to think about them for a bit. Lucky for you, here's a chance to do just that!

1. Try to determine the part of speech. What part of speech does it *feel* like to you?
2. Do your best to come up with a brief definition.

adumbrate
Part of Speech: n. v. adj. adv.

*Definition:*_____

_____

borborygmus
Part of Speech: n. v. adj. adv.

*Definition:*_____

_____

fuliginous
Part of Speech: n. v. adj. adv.

*Definition:*_____

_____

iconoclast
Part of Speech: n. v. adj. adv.

*Definition:*_____

_____

infelicitous
Part of Speech: n. v. adj. adv.

*Definition:*_____

_____

lachrymose
Part of Speech: n. v. adj. adv.

*Definition:*_____

_____

lycanthropy
Part of Speech: n. v. adj. adv.

*Definition:*_____

_____

milquetoast
Part of Speech: n. v. adj. adv.

*Definition:*_____

_____

mulct
Part of Speech: n. v. adj. adv.

*Definition:*_____

_____

omphaloskepsis
Part of Speech: n. v. adj. adv.

*Definition:*_____

_____

outré
Part of Speech: n. v. adj. adv.

*Definition:*_____

_____

pertinacious
Part of Speech: n. v. adj. adv.

*Definition:*_____

_____

recidivism
Part of Speech: n. v. adj. adv.

*Definition:*_____

_____

sesquipedalian
Part of Speech: n. v. adj. adv.

*Definition:*_____

_____

adumbrate

ad·um·brate • [ADD-um-brate] • \ ˈa-dəm-ˌbrāt \

- **verb**
    1. *to suggest, disclose, or outline partially*
    2. *to overshadow and obscure something*

My difficulties with the homework **adumbrated** a poor performance on the test.

SYNONYMS

ANTONYMS

WRITING TIME!
Use *adumbrate* in an original sentence of your own creation.

BONUS FUN TIME!
Express *adumbrate* with a drawing or
invent a dictionary-style definition of your own.

borborygmus

bor·bo·ryg·mus • [bawr-buh-RIG-muhs] • \ ˌbȯr-bə-ˈrig-məs \

- noun

a rumbling or gurgling sound caused by the movement of gas in the intestines

That chili cheese dog caused quite the **borborygmus** in my tummy.

SYNONYMS

ANTONYMS

WRITING TIME!
Use *borborygmus* in an original sentence of your own creation.

BONUS FUN TIME!
Express *borborygmus* with a drawing or
invent a dictionary-style definition of your own.

fuliginous

fu·lig·i·nous • [fyoo-LIJ-i-ness] • \ fyu̇-ˈli-jə-nəs \

- **adjective**
    1. *having the color or consistency of soot or smoke*
    2. *like soot in cloudiness or obscurity*

I can hardly see through the **fuliginous** window above the grill.

SYNONYMS

ANTONYMS

WRITING TIME!

Use *fuliginous* in an original sentence of your own creation.

BONUS FUN TIME!

Express *fuliginous* with a drawing or
invent a dictionary-style definition of your own.

iconoclast

i·con·o·clast • [eye-KON-uh-klast] • \ ī-ˈkä-nə-ˌklast \

- noun

somebody who challenges or overturns traditional beliefs, customs, and values

A true **iconoclast**, Mrs. Swarthmore was not afraid to challenge the school's teaching philosophies.

SYNONYMS

ANTONYMS

WRITING TIME!

Use *iconoclast* in an original sentence of your own creation.

BONUS FUN TIME!

Express *iconoclast* with a drawing or
invent a dictionary-style definition of your own.

infelicitous

in·fe·lic·i·tous • [in-fi-LIS-i-tes] • \ ˌin-fi-ˈli-sə-təs \

- adjective
> 1. inappropriate; ill-chosen
> 2. not happy; unfortunate

We received the **infelicitous** news of our favorite team's defeat.

SYNONYMS

ANTONYMS

WRITING TIME!

Use *infelicitous* in an original sentence of your own creation.

BONUS FUN TIME!

Express *infelicitous* with a drawing or
invent a dictionary-style definition of your own.

lachrymose

lach·ry·mose • [LAK-rah-mos] • \ ˈla-krə-ˌmōs \

> **- adjective**
> 1. *weeping or inclined to weep; tearful*
> 2. *causing or tending to cause tears*
>
> I felt **lachrymose** for an entire week after my favorite team lost the big game.

SYNONYMS

ANTONYMS

WRITING TIME!
Use *lachrymose* in an original sentence of your own creation.

BONUS FUN TIME!
Express *lachrymose* with a drawing or
invent a dictionary-style definition of your own.

lycanthropy

ly·can·thro·py • [LIE-kan-thro-pee] • \ lī-ˈkan(t)-thrə-pē \

> **- noun**
>
> *the delusion that one has become or has assumed the characteristics of a wolf*
>
> Sasha's little brother is currently suffering from **lycanthropy**; he spends most of the night howling at the moon.

SYNONYMS

ANTONYMS

WRITING TIME!

Use *lycanthropy* in an original sentence of your own creation.

BONUS FUN TIME!

Express *lycanthropy* with a drawing or
invent a dictionary-style definition of your own.

milquetoast

milque·toast • [MILK-toast] • \ ˈmilk-ˌtōst \

- noun

one who has a meek, timid, unassertive nature

Keisha knew that she would never get what she wanted if she kept being such a **milquetoast**.

SYNONYMS

ANTONYMS

WRITING TIME!

Use *milquetoast* in an original sentence of your own creation.

BONUS FUN TIME!

Express *milquetoast* with a drawing or
invent a dictionary-style definition of your own.

mulct

mulct • [MULKT] • \ ˈməlkt \

- verb

1. *to acquire by trickery or deception*
2. *to swindle or defraud*

The con man **mukcts** unsuspecting victims to get what he wants.

SYNONYMS

ANTONYMS

WRITING TIME!

Use *mulct* in an original sentence of your own creation.

BONUS FUN TIME!

Express *mulct* with a drawing or
invent a dictionary-style definition of your own.

omphaloskepsis

om·pha·lo·skep·sis • [om-fah-loh-SKEP-sis] • \ ˌäm(p)-fə-lō-ˈskep-səs \

- noun

the contemplation of one's navel; navel-gazing

People today are so engaged in **omphaloskepsis** that they hardly care about the world around them.

SYNONYMS

ANTONYMS

WRITING TIME!
Use *omphaloskepsis* in an original sentence of your own creation.

BONUS FUN TIME!
Express *omphaloskepsis* with a drawing or
invent a dictionary-style definition of your own.

outré

ou·tré • [oo-TRAY] • \ ü-ˈtrā \

- adjective

passing well beyond what is usual, normal, or generally acceptable

That comedian crossed the line with some truly **outré** jokes.

SYNONYMS

ANTONYMS

WRITING TIME!
Use *outré* in an original sentence of your own creation.

BONUS FUN TIME!
Express *outré* with a drawing or
invent a dictionary-style definition of your own.

pertinacious

per·ti·na·cious • [per-tih-NAY-shuss] • \ ˌpər-tə-ˈnā-shəs \

- adjective
1. *determinedly resolute in purpose, belief, or action*
2. *highly persistent*

I didn't know at first, but I was **pertinacious** enough that I finally figured it out.

SYNONYMS

ANTONYMS

WRITING TIME!
Use *pertinacious* in an original sentence of your own creation.

BONUS FUN TIME!
Express *pertinacious* with a drawing or
invent a dictionary-style definition of your own.

recidivism

re·cid·i·vis·m   •   [rih-SID-ih-viz-um]   •   \ ri-ˈsi-də-ˌvi-zəm \

> **- noun**
>
> *the tendency to relapse into a previous undesirable type of behavior, especially crime*
>
> **Recidivism** can be a real challenge for those recently released from prison.

SYNONYMS

ANTONYMS

WRITING TIME!
Use *recidivism* in an original sentence of your own creation.

BONUS FUN TIME!
Express *recidivism* with a drawing or
invent a dictionary-style definition of your own.

sesquipedalian

ses·qui·pe·da·li·an • [ses-quih-puh-DAY-lee-un] • \ ˌse-skwə-pə-ˈdāl-yən \

- adjective
   1. *characterized by the use of very long words*
   2. *relating to or being a long word*

Your writing is overly **sesquipedalian**, so please use shorter words for clarity.

SYNONYMS

ANTONYMS

WRITING TIME!
Use *sesquipedalian* in an original sentence of your own creation.

BONUS FUN TIME!
Express *sesquipedalian* with a drawing or
invent a dictionary-style definition of your own.

Section Two: Word Review

Congratulations on learning fourteen more amazing words! Remember that the whole point of learning new vocabulary is to actually use it, so let's put your new vocabulary to use.

1. Review the words you've learned. Consider what comes to mind when you say the words themselves. How about when you read the definitions?
2. Circle at least **three** of your favorites. You'll get to use these in your very own story.

adumbrate —— verb
1. to suggest, disclose, or outline partially
2. to overshadow and obscure something

borborygmus —— noun
a rumbling or gurgling sound caused by the movement of gas in the intestines

fuliginous —— adjective
1. having the color or consistency of soot or smoke
2. like soot in cloudiness or obscurity

iconoclast —— noun
somebody who challenges or overturns traditional beliefs, customs, and values

infelicitous —— adjective
1. inappropriate; ill-chosen
2. not happy; unfortunate

lachrymose —— adjective
1. weeping or inclined to weep; tearful
2. causing or tending to cause tears.

lycanthropy —— noun
the delusion that one has become or has assumed the characteristics of a wolf

milquetoast —— noun
one who has a meek, timid, unassertive nature

mulct —— verb
1. to acquire by trickery or deception
2. to swindle or defraud

omphaloskepsis —— noun
the contemplation of one's navel; navel-gazing

outré —— adjective
passing well beyond what is usual, normal, or generally acceptable

pertinacious —— adjective
1. determinedly resolute in purpose, belief, or action
2. highly persistent

recidivism —— noun
the tendency to relapse into a previous undesirable type of behavior, especially crime

sesquipedalian — adjective
1. characterized by the use of very long words
2. relating to or being a long word

STORY TWO

1. List the words you've chosen:

_____

2. Write a story that incorporates all of your chosen words. If you can't think of anything to write about, consider these suggestions:
   - Write a story in which your main character is allergic to water.
   - Write a journal entry about a pet you've always wanted.

Title:_____

_____

_____

_____

_____

_____

_____

_____

_____

_____

_____

SECTION THREE: WORD PREVIEW
Welcome to your fourteen new favorite words!

When you encounter new words, it's a good idea to think about them for a bit. Lucky for you, here's a chance to do just that!

1. Try to determine the part of speech. What part of speech does it *feel* like to you?
2. Do your best to come up with a brief definition.

—— alexithymia ——
Part of Speech: n. v. adj. adv.

*Definition:*_____

_____

—— anfractuous ——
Part of Speech: n. v. adj. adv.

*Definition:*_____

_____

—— cerebellum ——
Part of Speech: n. v. adj. adv.

*Definition:*_____

_____

—— discombobulate ——
Part of Speech: n. v. adj. adv.

*Definition:*_____

_____

—— ebullition ——
Part of Speech: n. v. adj. adv.

*Definition:*_____

_____

—— hebetudinous ——
Part of Speech: n. v. adj. adv.

*Definition:*_____

_____

—— hemidemisemiquaver ——
Part of Speech: n. v. adj. adv.

*Definition:*_____

_____

—— kakistocracy ——
Part of Speech: n. v. adj. adv.

*Definition:*_____

_____

—— multifarious ——
Part of Speech: n. v. adj. adv.

*Definition:*_____

_____

—— paroxysm ——
Part of Speech: n. v. adj. adv.

*Definition:*_____

_____

—— recherché ——
Part of Speech: n. v. adj. adv.

*Definition:*_____

_____

—— schadenfreude ——
Part of Speech: n. v. adj. adv.

*Definition:*_____

_____

—— ululate ——
Part of Speech: n. v. adj. adv.

*Definition:*_____

_____

—— vertiginous ——
Part of Speech: n. v. adj. adv.

*Definition:*_____

_____

alexithymia

a·lex·i·thy·mi·a • [ey-lek-suh-THAHY-mee-uh] • \ ə-ˌleks-i-ˈthī-mē-ə \

- noun

difficulty in experiencing, expressing, and describing emotional responses

My **alexithymia** makes it hard for me to talk about my feelings.

SYNONYMS

ANTONYMS

WRITING TIME!

Use *alexithymia* in an original sentence of your own creation.

BONUS FUN TIME!

Express *alexithymia* with a drawing or
invent a dictionary-style definition of your own.

anfractuous

an·frac·tu·ous • [an-FRACK-choo-wuss] • \ an-ˈfrak-chə-wəs \

- adjective

with much twisting and turning; full of windings and intricacies

The best part of that mystery novel was that **anfractuous** storyline.

SYNONYMS

ANTONYMS

WRITING TIME!
Use *anfractuous* in an original sentence of your own creation.

BONUS FUN TIME!
Express *anfractuous* with a drawing or
invent a dictionary-style definition of your own.

cerebellum

cer·e·bel·lum • [sare-uh-BELL-um] • \ ˌser-ə-ˈbe-ləm \

> **- noun**
>
> *the part of the brain with the main function of controlling and coordinating muscular activity and maintaining balance*
>
> There must be something wrong with my **cerebellum**; I keep tripping!

SYNONYMS

ANTONYMS

WRITING TIME!
Use *cerebellum* in an original sentence of your own creation.

BONUS FUN TIME!
Express *cerebellum* with a drawing or
invent a dictionary-style definition of your own.

discombobulate

dis·com·bob·u·late • [dis-kom-BOB-yoo-late] • \ ˌdis-kəm-ˈbä-b(y)ə-ˌlāt \

- verb

to confuse or disconcert; upset; frustrate

My coach **discombobulated** me by giving me a lot of instruction all at once.

SYNONYMS

ANTONYMS

WRITING TIME!
Use *discombobulate* in an original sentence of your own creation.

BONUS FUN TIME!
Express *discombobulate* with a drawing or
invent a dictionary-style definition of your own.

ebullition

eb·ul·li·tion • [ebb-uh-LISH-un] • \ ˌe-bə-ˈli-shən \

- noun

    1. a state of bubbling up or boiling
    2. a sudden outbreak of violent emotion

I tried to control myself when the bullies taunted me, but I couldn't keep my **ebullition** in check.

SYNONYMS

ANTONYMS

WRITING TIME!
Use *ebullition* in an original sentence of your own creation.

BONUS FUN TIME!
Express *ebullition* with a drawing or
invent a dictionary-style definition of your own.

hebetudinous

heb·e·tud·i·nous • [heb-i-TOOD-i-niss] • \ ˌhe-bə-ˈtü-dᵊn-əs \

- adjective

dull-minded; mentally lethargic

Our teacher prefers insightful students to **hebetudinous** ones.

SYNONYMS

ANTONYMS

WRITING TIME!
Use *hebetudinous* in an original sentence of your own creation.

BONUS FUN TIME!
Express *hebetudinous* with a drawing or
invent a dictionary-style definition of your own.

hemidemisemiquaver

he·mi·de·mi·se·mi·qua·ver ● [hem-ee-dem-ee-SEM-ee-kwa-ver] ● \ ˌhe-mi-ˌde-mi-ˈse-mi-ˌkwā-vər \

- noun

one sixty-fourth musical note

I am just learning piano, so playing a piece that includes **hemidemisemiquavers** is too difficult for me.

SYNONYMS

ANTONYMS

WRITING TIME!
Use *hemidemisemiquaver* in an original sentence of your own creation.

BONUS FUN TIME!
Express *hemidemisemiquaver* with a drawing or
invent a dictionary-style definition of your own.

kakistocracy

kak·is·toc·ra·cy • [kak-i-STOK-rah-see] • \ ˌka-kə-ˈstä-krə-sē \

- noun

government by the worst or least qualified citizens

Smart and qualified people must run for public office so that our country doesn't become a **kakistocracy**.

Synonyms

Antonyms

Writing Time!

Use *kakistocracy* in an original sentence of your own creation.

Bonus Fun Time!

Express *kakistocracy* with a drawing or
invent a dictionary-style definition of your own.

multifarious

mul·ti·far·i·ous • [mul-tih-FARE-ee-uss] • \ ˌməl-tə-ˈfer-ē-əs \

- **adjective**

including parts, things, or people of many different kinds

The **multifarious** gears of a pocket watch are fascinating to me.

SYNONYMS

ANTONYMS

WRITING TIME!
Use *multifarious* in an original sentence of your own creation.

BONUS FUN TIME!
Express *multifarious* with a drawing or
invent a dictionary-style definition of your own.

paroxysm

par·ox·ys·m • [PARE-uk-siz-um] • \ ˈper-ək-ˌsi-zəm \

> **- noun**
>
> *a sudden and uncontrollable expression of emotion*
>
> The audience burst into a collective **paroxysm** at the end of *Romeo & Juliet*.

SYNONYMS

ANTONYMS

WRITING TIME!
Use *paroxysm* in an original sentence of your own creation.

BONUS FUN TIME!
Express *paroxysm* with a drawing or
invent a dictionary-style definition of your own.

recherché

re·cher·ché • [rah-sher-SHAY] • \ rə-ˌsher-ˈshā \

- **adjective**
    1. *uncommon; rare*
    2. *pretentious; overblown*

That artist uses techniques that have become **recherché** in recent years.

SYNONYMS

ANTONYMS

WRITING TIME!
Use *recherché* in an original sentence of your own creation.

BONUS FUN TIME!
Express *recherché* with a drawing or
invent a dictionary-style definition of your own.

schadenfreude

scha·den·freu·de • [SHAH-dun-froy-duh] • \ ˈshä-dᵊn-ˌfrȯi-də \

> **- noun**
>
> *enjoyment obtained from the troubles of others*
>
> I couldn't help feeling **schadenfreude** when the bully tripped on the curb and dropped his ice cream cone on the sidewalk.

SYNONYMS

ANTONYMS

WRITING TIME!
Use *schadenfreude* in an original sentence of your own creation.

BONUS FUN TIME!
Express *schadenfreude* with a drawing or
invent a dictionary-style definition of your own.

ululate

ul·u·late • [UHL-yuh-layt] • \ ˈəl-yə-ˌlāt \

- verb

> *to howl, wail, or lament loudly*

My sister tends to **ululate** when things don't go her way.

SYNONYMS

ANTONYMS

WRITING TIME!

Use *ululate* in an original sentence of your own creation.

BONUS FUN TIME!

Express *ululate* with a drawing or
invent a dictionary-style definition of your own.

vertiginous

ver·tig·i·nous • [ver-TIJ-uh-nuss] • \ vər-ˈti-jə-nəs \

- adjective

1. causing dizziness, especially because of being very high or exposed

2. relating to or suffering from the whirling or tilting sensation of vertigo

Molly felt ill when she looked at the **vertiginous** view from the top of the pyramid.

SYNONYMS

ANTONYMS

WRITING TIME!

Use *vertiginous* in an original sentence of your own creation.

BONUS FUN TIME!

Express *vertiginous* with a drawing or
invent a dictionary-style definition of your own.

Section Three: Word Review

Congratulations on learning fourteen more amazing words! Remember that the whole point of learning new vocabulary is to actually use it, so let's put your new vocabulary to use.

1. Review the words you've learned. Consider what comes to mind when you say the words themselves. How about when you read the definitions?
2. Circle at least **three** of your favorites. You'll get to use these in your very own story.

alexithymia — noun
difficulty in experiencing, expressing, and describing emotional responses

anfractuous — adjective
with much twisting and turning; full of windings and intricacies

cerebellum — noun
the part of the brain with the main function of coordinating muscular activity and maintaining balance

discombobulate — verb
to confuse or disconcert; upset; frustrate

ebullition — noun
1. a state of bubbling up or boiling
2. a sudden outbreak of violent emotion

hebetudinous — adjective
dull-minded; mentally lethargic

hemidemisemiquaver · noun
one sixty-fourth musical note

kakistocracy — noun
government by the worst or least qualified citizens

multifarious — adjective
including parts, things, or people of many different kinds

paroxysm — noun
a sudden and uncontrollable expression of emotion

recherché — adjective
1. uncommon; rare
2. exquisite; choice
3. pretentious; overblown

schadenfreude — noun
enjoyment obtained from the troubles of others

ululate — verb
to howl, wail, or lament loudly

vertiginous — adjective
1. causing dizziness, especially because of being very high or exposed
2. relating to sensation of vertigo

STORY THREE

1. List the words you've chosen:

_____

2. Write a story that incorporates all of your chosen words. If you can't think of anything to write about, consider these suggestions:
   - Write a story in which one of your main character's five senses is heightened.
   - Write a story in which your main character wakes up unexpectedly unable to speak the local language.

Title: _____

_____

_____

_____

_____

_____

_____

_____

_____

_____

_____

SECTION FOUR: WORD PREVIEW
Welcome to your fourteen new favorite words!

When you encounter new words, it's a good idea to think about them for a bit. Lucky for you, here's a chance to do just that!

1. Try to determine the part of speech. What part of speech does it *feel* like to you?
2. Do your best to come up with a brief definition.

abecedarian
Part of Speech: n. v. adj. adv.

Definition:_____

_____

brummagem
Part of Speech: n. v. adj. adv.

Definition:_____

_____

eleemosynary
Part of Speech: n. v. adj. adv.

Definition:_____

_____

energumen
Part of Speech: n. v. adj. adv.

Definition:_____

_____

inveigle
Part of Speech: n. v. adj. adv.

Definition:_____

_____

jejune
Part of Speech: n. v. adj. adv.

Definition:_____

_____

juvenescent
Part of Speech: n. v. adj. adv.

Definition:_____

_____

kerfuffle
Part of Speech: n. v. adj. adv.

Definition:_____

_____

machination
Part of Speech: n. v. adj. adv.

Definition:_____

_____

pandiculation
Part of Speech: n. v. adj. adv.

Definition:_____

_____

peripatetic
Part of Speech: n. v. adj. adv.

Definition:_____

_____

rodomontade
Part of Speech: n. v. adj. adv.

Definition:_____

_____

stentorian
Part of Speech: n. v. adj. adv.

Definition:_____

_____

tintinnabulation
Part of Speech: n. v. adj. adv.

Definition:_____

_____

abecedarian

a·be·ce·dar·i·an • [ay-bee-see-DARE-ee-un] • \ ˌā-bē-(ˌ)sē-ˈder-ē-ən \

- noun

somebody who is learning the basics of a subject

Even the most accomplished expert was an **abecedarian** at one point.

SYNONYMS

ANTONYMS

WRITING TIME!
Use *abecedarian* in an original sentence of your own creation.

BONUS FUN TIME!
Express *abecedarian* with a drawing or
invent a dictionary-style definition of your own.

brummagem

brum·ma·gem • [BRUHM-uh-juhm] • \ ˈbrə-mi-jəm \

- noun

something, especially imitation jewelry, that is cheap and gaudy

My favorite **brummagem** in the costume shop was an enormous fake diamond necklace.

SYNONYMS

ANTONYMS

WRITING TIME!
Use *brummagem* in an original sentence of your own creation.

BONUS FUN TIME!
Express *brummagem* with a drawing or
invent a dictionary-style definition of your own.

eleemosynary

el·ee·mo·sy·na·ry • [eh-lee-MAHSS-uh-nair-ee] • \ ˌe-li-ˈmä-sə-ˌner-ē \

- adjective

relating to or given as charity

Sara's effort at the food bank was **eleemosynary**, so she didn't expect to be paid.

SYNONYMS

ANTONYMS

WRITING TIME!
Use *eleemosynary* in an original sentence of your own creation.

BONUS FUN TIME!
Express *eleemosynary* with a drawing or
invent a dictionary-style definition of your own.

energumen

en·er·gu·men • [en-er-GU-men] • \ ˌenə(r)ˈgyümən \

- noun

one who is possessed by a demonic entity

Amelia's favorite video game involves fighting off evil spirits and trying not to become an **energumen**.

SYNONYMS

ANTONYMS

WRITING TIME!

Use *energumen* in an original sentence of your own creation.

BONUS FUN TIME!

Express *energumen* with a drawing or
invent a dictionary-style definition of your own.

inveigle

in·vei·gle • [in-VAY-gul] • \ in-ˈvā-gəl \

- verb

to charm or entice somebody into doing something they would not otherwise have done

A good con artist **inveigles** people to do just about anything.

SYNONYMS

ANTONYMS

WRITING TIME!

Use *inveigle* in an original sentence of your own creation.

BONUS FUN TIME!

Express *inveigle* with a drawing or
invent a dictionary-style definition of your own.

jejune

je·june • [jeh-JOON] • \ ji-ˈjün \

- adjective

dull, empty; childish

We had to sit through another one of my sister's **jejune** lectures about the color periwinkle.

SYNONYMS

ANTONYMS

WRITING TIME!

Use *jejune* in an original sentence of your own creation.

BONUS FUN TIME!

Express *jejune* with a drawing or
invent a dictionary-style definition of your own.

juvenescent

ju·ve·nes·cent　•　[joo-vah-NES-ent]　•　\ jü-və-ˈne-sᵊnt \

- adjective

becoming young or youthful

A quick dip in the freezing river left me feeling refreshed and **juvenescent**.

SYNONYMS

ANTONYMS

WRITING TIME!

Use *juvenescent* in an original sentence of your own creation.

BONUS FUN TIME!

Express *juvenescent* with a drawing or
invent a dictionary-style definition of your own.

kerfuffle

ker·fuf·fle • [ker-FUF-el] • \ kər-ˈfə-fəl \

- noun

a disorderly outburst or tumult

The release of the new video game console caused quite a **kerfuffle** at the electronics store.

SYNONYMS

ANTONYMS

WRITING TIME!

Use *kerfuffle* in an original sentence of your own creation.

BONUS FUN TIME!

Express *kerfuffle* with a drawing or
invent a dictionary-style definition of your own.

machination

mach·i·na·tion • [mak-uh-NAY-shun] • \ ˌma-kə-ˈnā-shən \

- noun

  1. *the devising of secret, cunning, or complicated plans and schemes*
  2. *a secret, cunning, or complicated plan designed to achieve a particular end*

Nobody could have anticipated the villain's **machination**, which made the movie so exciting.

SYNONYMS

ANTONYMS

WRITING TIME!

Use *machination* in an original sentence of your own creation.

BONUS FUN TIME!

Express *machination* with a drawing or
invent a dictionary-style definition of your own.

pandiculation

pan·dic·u·la·tion • [pan-dik-yoo-LAY-shen] • \ pan-ˌdik-yə-ˈlā-shən \

- noun

yawning and stretching (as when first waking up)

There's nothing quite as cute as the **pandiculation** of a little kitten.

SYNONYMS

ANTONYMS

WRITING TIME!

Use *pandiculation* in an original sentence of your own creation.

BONUS FUN TIME!

Express *pandiculation* with a drawing or
invent a dictionary-style definition of your own.

peripatetic

per·i·pa·tet·ic • [per-ih-puh-TET-ik] • \ ˌper-ə-pə-ˈte-tik \

- adjective

traveling from place to place, especially working in several establishments and traveling between them

My life is too **peripatetic** these days; I just wish I had my own office.

SYNONYMS

ANTONYMS

WRITING TIME!

Use *peripatetic* in an original sentence of your own creation.

BONUS FUN TIME!

Express *peripatetic* with a drawing or
invent a dictionary-style definition of your own.

rodomontade

ro·do·mon·tade • [rod-ah-mon-TADE] • \ ˌrä-də-mən-ˈtād \

- noun

pretentious boasting or bragging; bluster

It's true that my brother is a very good skier, but I'm sick of listening to his constant **rodomontade** about it.

SYNONYMS

ANTONYMS

WRITING TIME!
Use *rodomontade* in an original sentence of your own creation.

BONUS FUN TIME!
Express *rodomontade* with a drawing or
invent a dictionary-style definition of your own.

stentorian

sten·to·ri·an • [sten-TOR-ee-en] • \ sten-ˈtȯr-ē-ən \

- adjective

very loud or powerful in sound

It was impossible to ignore the **stentorian** roars from the approaching grizzly bear.

SYNONYMS

ANTONYMS

WRITING TIME!

Use *stentorian* in an original sentence of your own creation.

BONUS FUN TIME!

Express *stentorian* with a drawing or
invent a dictionary-style definition of your own.

tintinnabulation

tin·tin·nab·u·la·tion • [tin-ti-nab-yoo-LAY-shen] • \ ˌtin-tə-ˌna-byə-ˈlā-shən \

> **- noun**
>
> *the ringing or sounding of bells*
>
> The church bells' intricate **tintinnabulation** let us know it was time to go inside.

SYNONYMS

ANTONYMS

WRITING TIME!
Use *tintinnabulation* in an original sentence of your own creation.

BONUS FUN TIME!
Express *tintinnabulation* with a drawing or
invent a dictionary-style definition of your own.

SECTION FOUR: WORD REVIEW

Congratulations on learning fourteen more amazing words! Remember that the whole point of learning new vocabulary is to actually use it, so let's put your new vocabulary to use.

1. Review the words you've learned. Consider what comes to mind when you say the words themselves. How about when you read the definitions?

2. Circle at least **three** of your favorites. You'll get to use these in your very own story.

abecedarian —————— noun
somebody who is learning the basics of literacy or a subject

brummagem —————— noun
something, especially imitation jewelry, that is cheap and gaudy

eleemosynary —— adjective
relating to or given as charity

energumen —————— noun
one who is possessed by a demonic entity

inveigle —————— verb
to charm or entice somebody into doing something that he or she would not otherwise have done

jejune —————— adjective
dull, empty; childish

juvenescent —— adjective
becoming young or youthful

kerfuffle —————— noun
a disorderly outburst or tumult

machination —————— noun
1. the devising of secret, cunning, or complicated plans and schemes

pandiculation —————— noun
yawning and stretching (as when first waking up).

peripatetic —— adjective
traveling from place to place, especially working in several establishments and traveling between them

rodomontade —————— noun
pretentious boasting or bragging; bluster

stentorian —— adjective
very loud or powerful in sound

tintinnabulation —— noun
the ringing or sounding of bells

STORY FOUR

1. List the words you've chosen:

_____

2. Write a story that incorporates all of your chosen words. If you can't think of anything to write about, consider these suggestions:
   - Write a story in which you meet your hero.
   - Write a story in which your main character finds an unmarked suitcase with $1,000,000 in cash inside.

Title:_____

_____

_____

_____

_____

_____

_____

_____

_____

_____

Section Five: Word Preview
Welcome to your fourteen new favorite words!

When you encounter new words, it's a good idea to think about them for a bit. Lucky for you, here's a chance to do just that!

1. Try to determine the part of speech. What part of speech does it *feel* like to you?
2. Do your best to come up with a brief definition.

bumptious
Part of Speech: n. v. adj. adv.

*Definition:*_____

_____

cognoscente
Part of Speech: n. v. adj. adv.

*Definition:*_____

_____

contumely
Part of Speech: n. v. adj. adv.

*Definition:*_____

_____

defenestrate
Part of Speech: n. v. adj. adv.

*Definition:*_____

_____

farouche
Part of Speech: n. v. adj. adv.

*Definition:*_____

_____

gimcrackery
Part of Speech: n. v. adj. adv.

*Definition:*_____

_____

idoneous
Part of Speech: n. v. adj. adv.

*Definition:*_____

_____

imbroglio
Part of Speech: n. v. adj. adv.

*Definition:*_____

_____

metonymy
Part of Speech: n. v. adj. adv.

*Definition:*_____

_____

noctilucous
Part of Speech: n. v. adj. adv.

*Definition:*_____

_____

ochlophobia
Part of Speech: n. v. adj. adv.

*Definition:*_____

_____

quiescent
Part of Speech: n. v. adj. adv.

*Definition:*_____

_____

quotidian
Part of Speech: n. v. adj. adv.

*Definition:*_____

_____

sangfroid
Part of Speech: n. v. adj. adv.

*Definition:*_____

_____

bumptious

bump·tious • [BUMP-shuss] • \ ˈbəm(p)-shəs \

- adjective

stating opinions aggressively or self-importantly

I wish you would listen more instead of being so **bumptious** all the time.

SYNONYMS

ANTONYMS

WRITING TIME!
Use *bumptious* in an original sentence of your own creation.

BONUS FUN TIME!
Express *bumptious* with a drawing or
invent a dictionary-style definition of your own.

cognoscente

co·gno·scen·te • [kon-yuh-SHEN-tee] • \ ˌkän-yə-ˈshen-tē \

- **noun**

a person who has expert knowledge in a subject

If you're looking for useful information, it's best to ask a **cognoscente** about it.

SYNONYMS

ANTONYMS

WRITING TIME!
Use *cognoscente* in an original sentence of your own creation.

BONUS FUN TIME!
Express *cognoscente* with a drawing or
invent a dictionary-style definition of your own.

contumely

con·tu·me·ly • [KON-too-mah-lee] • \ kän-ˈtü-mə-lē \

- **noun**

rudeness or contempt arising from haughtiness; insolence

Your **contumely** will not be tolerated here, so please be more polite.

SYNONYMS

ANTONYMS

WRITING TIME!
Use *contumely* in an original sentence of your own creation.

BONUS FUN TIME!
Express *contumely* with a drawing or
invent a dictionary-style definition of your own.

defenestrate

de·fen·es·trate • [dee-FEN-i-strate] • \ dē-ˈfe-nə-ˌstrāt \

- verb

to throw out of a window

Ryan **defenestrated** the spider back outside instead of squashing it.

SYNONYMS

ANTONYMS

WRITING TIME!

Use *defenestrate* in an original sentence of your own creation.

BONUS FUN TIME!

Express *defenestrate* with a drawing or
invent a dictionary-style definition of your own.

farouche

fa·rouche • [fuh-ROOSH] • \ fə-ˈrüsh \

- **adjective**

 unsociable and lacking grace because of fierceness, sullenness, or shyness

 My brother is so **farouche** these days that we can't really take him to dinner parties.

SYNONYMS

ANTONYMS

WRITING TIME!

Use *farouche* in an original sentence of your own creation.

BONUS FUN TIME!

Express *farouche* with a drawing or
invent a dictionary-style definition of your own.

gimcrackery

gim·crack·e·ry • [JIM-crack-ur-ee] • \ ˈjim-ˌkra-kə-rē \

- **noun**

a showy object or objects of little use or value

What looked like valuable treasure was actually nothing but useless **gimcrackery**.

SYNONYMS

ANTONYMS

WRITING TIME!

Use *gimcrackery* in an original sentence of your own creation.

BONUS FUN TIME!

Express *gimcrackery* with a drawing or
invent a dictionary-style definition of your own.

idoneous

i·do·ne·ous • [i-DOE-nee-es] • \ (')ī¦dōnēəs \

- **adjective**

appropriate; suitable; adequate

We spent over an hour looking for an **idoneous** place to set up camp.

SYNONYMS

ANTONYMS

WRITING TIME!

Use *idoneous* in an original sentence of your own creation.

BONUS FUN TIME!

Express *idoneous* with a drawing or
invent a dictionary-style definition of your own.

imbroglio

im·bro·gli·o • [im-BROA-lee-o] • \ im-ˈbrōl-(ˌ)yō \

> **- noun**
>
> *a confusing, messy, or complicated situation, especially one that involves disagreement or intrigue*
>
> The first rule of middle school is not to get involved in any friendship **imbroglio**.

SYNONYMS

ANTONYMS

WRITING TIME!
Use *imbroglio* in an original sentence of your own creation.

BONUS FUN TIME!
Express *imbroglio* with a drawing or
invent a dictionary-style definition of your own.

metonymy

me·ton·y·my • [mih-TAHN-uh-mee] • \ mə-ˈtä-nə-mē \

- noun

a figure of speech in which an attribute of something is used to stand for the thing itself, such as "suit" for businessperson.

"The pen is mightier than the sword" is a phrase with two uses of **metonymy**.

SYNONYMS

ANTONYMS

WRITING TIME!
Use *metonymy* in an original sentence of your own creation.

BONUS FUN TIME!
Express *metonymy* with a drawing or
invent a dictionary-style definition of your own.

noctilucous

noc·ti·lu·cous • [nok-ti-LYOO-kes] • \ noc-`ti- lu"cous \

- adjective

shining in the night

My flashlight briefly passed over the **noctilucous** eyes of the jaguar in the tree above me.

SYNONYMS

ANTONYMS

WRITING TIME!
Use *noctilucous* in an original sentence of your own creation.

BONUS FUN TIME!
Express *noctilucous* with a drawing or
invent a dictionary-style definition of your own.

ochlophobia

och·lo·pho·bi·a • [ok-luh-FO-be-uh] • \ ˌäk-lə-ˈfō-bē-ə \

- noun

an abnormal fear of crowds

Due to my **ochlophobia**, I prefer to watch large sporting events on television.

SYNONYMS

ANTONYMS

WRITING TIME!

Use *ochlophobia* in an original sentence of your own creation.

BONUS FUN TIME!

Express *ochlophobia* with a drawing or
invent a dictionary-style definition of your own.

quiescent

qui·es·cent • [kwee-ESS-unt] • \ kwī-ˈe-sᵊnt \

- adjective

inactive or at rest

The **quiescent** picnic-goers lounged in the shade of an enormous tree.

SYNONYMS

ANTONYMS

WRITING TIME!

Use *quiescent* in an original sentence of your own creation.

BONUS FUN TIME!

Express *quiescent* with a drawing or
invent a dictionary-style definition of your own.

quotidian

quo·tid·i·an　•　[kwo-TID-ee-an]　•　\ kwō-ˈti-dē-ən \

- adjective

daily; everyday; commonplace

Eleanor ordered a **quotidian** burger and fries, but I asked for something special that wasn't on the menu.

SYNONYMS

ANTONYMS

WRITING TIME!
Use *quotidian* in an original sentence of your own creation.

BONUS FUN TIME!
Express *quotidian* with a drawing or
invent a dictionary-style definition of your own.

sangfroid

sang·froid • [san-FRWA] • \ ˌsäŋ-ˈf(r)wä \

- **noun**

self-possession or imperturbability especially under strain

The captain's **sangfroid** was both impressive and reassuring during the difficult

SYNONYMS

ANTONYMS

WRITING TIME!
Use *sangfroid* in an original sentence of your own creation.

BONUS FUN TIME!
Express *sangfroid* with a drawing or
invent a dictionary-style definition of your own.

SECTION FIVE: WORD REVIEW

Congratulations on learning fourteen more amazing words! Remember that the whole point of learning new vocabulary is to actually use it, so let's put your new vocabulary to use.

1. Review the words you've learned. Consider what comes to mind when you say the words themselves. How about when you read the definitions?
2. Circle at least **three** of your favorites. You'll get to use these in your very own story.

bumptious ——— adjective

stating opinions aggressively or self-importantly

cognoscente ——— noun

a person who has expert knowledge in a subject

contumely ——— noun

rudeness or contempt arising from haughtiness; insolence

defenestrate ——— verb

to throw out of a window

farouche ——— adjective

unsociable and lacking grace because of fierceness, sullenness, or shyness

gimcrackery ——— noun

a showy object or objects of little use or value

idoneous ——— adjective

appropriate; suitable; adequate

imbroglio ——— noun

a confusing, messy, or complicated situation, especially one that involves disagreement or intrigue

metonymy ——— noun

a figure of speech in which an attribute of something is used to stand for the thing itself

noctilucous ——— adjective

shining in the night

ochlophobia ——— noun

an abnormal fear of crowds

quiescent ——— adjective

inactive or at rest

quotidian ——— adjective

daily; everyday; commonplace

sangfroid ——— noun

self-possession or imperturbability especially under strain

STORY FIVE

1. List the words you've chosen:

   _____

2. Write a story that incorporates all of your chosen words. If you can't think of anything to write about, consider these suggestions:
   - Write a story in which the main character is having the best day of their life.
   - Write a story involving a situation that makes you uncomfortable.

Title: _____

_____

_____

_____

_____

_____

_____

_____

_____

_____

_____

Section Six: Word Preview
Welcome to your fourteen new favorite words!

When you encounter new words, it's a good idea to think about them for a bit. Lucky for you, here's a chance to do just that!

1. Try to determine the part of speech. What part of speech does it *feel* like to you?
2. Do your best to come up with a brief definition.

amanuensis
Part of Speech: n. v. adj. adv.

Definition:_____

_____

chimerical
Part of Speech: n. v. adj. adv.

Definition:_____

_____

claque
Part of Speech: n. v. adj. adv.

Definition:_____

_____

exculpate
Part of Speech: n. v. adj. adv.

Definition:_____

_____

flapdoodle
Part of Speech: n. v. adj. adv.

Definition:_____

_____

insouciant
Part of Speech: n. v. adj. adv.

Definition:_____

_____

orotund
Part of Speech: n. v. adj. adv.

Definition:_____

_____

perambulate
Part of Speech: n. v. adj. adv.

Definition:_____

_____

perspicacious
Part of Speech: n. v. adj. adv.

Definition:_____

_____

quidnunc
Part of Speech: n. v. adj. adv.

Definition:_____

_____

redoubtable
Part of Speech: n. v. adj. adv.

Definition:_____

_____

skulduggery
Part of Speech: n. v. adj. adv.

Definition:_____

_____

somnolent
Part of Speech: n. v. adj. adv.

Definition:_____

_____

toothsome
Part of Speech: n. v. adj. adv.

Definition:_____

_____

amanuensis

a·man·u·en·sis • [uh-man-you-WHEN-suss] • \ ə-ˌman-yə-ˈwen(t)-səs \

> **- noun**
> 1. *somebody who takes dictation or copies manuscripts*
> 2. *a writer's assistant*
>
> My job as an **amanuensis** taught me a lot about writing.

SYNONYMS

ANTONYMS

WRITING TIME!
Use *amanuensis* in an original sentence of your own creation.

BONUS FUN TIME!
Express *amanuensis* with a drawing or
invent a dictionary-style definition of your own.

chimerical

chi·me·ri·cal   •   [kih-MARE-ih-kull]   •   \ kī-ˈmer-i-kəl \

- adjective

    1. wildly improbable or unrealistic
    2. having a tendency to indulge in unrealistic fantasies

I spend too much time setting **chimerical** goals when I should be focusing on what I can actually accomplish.

SYNONYMS

ANTONYMS

WRITING TIME!

Use *chimerical* in an original sentence of your own creation.

BONUS FUN TIME!

Express *chimerical* with a drawing or
invent a dictionary-style definition of your own.

claque

claque • [klak] • \ ˈklak \

- noun

a group of people hired to applaud a performance

The actor's **claque** made so much noise that it seemed as though the entire audience enjoyed his performance.

SYNONYMS

ANTONYMS

WRITING TIME!

Use *claque* in an original sentence of your own creation.

BONUS FUN TIME!

Express *claque* with a drawing or
invent a dictionary-style definition of your own.

exculpate

ex·cul·pate • [EK-skul-pate] • \ ˈek-(ˌ)skəl-ˌpāt \

- **verb**

to free somebody from blame or accusation of guilt

New DNA evidence **exculpated** the wrongly accused defendant.

SYNONYMS

ANTONYMS

WRITING TIME!
Use *exculpate* in an original sentence of your own creation.

BONUS FUN TIME!
Express *exculpate* with a drawing or
invent a dictionary-style definition of your own.

flapdoodle

flap·doo·dle • [FLAP-dood-el] • \ ˈflap-ˌdü-dᵊl \

- noun

foolish talk; nonsense

I'm sick of all this **flapdoodle**; I want to talk about things that matter.

SYNONYMS

ANTONYMS

WRITING TIME!

Use *flapdoodle* in an original sentence of your own creation.

BONUS FUN TIME!

Express *flapdoodle* with a drawing or
invent a dictionary-style definition of your own.

insouciant

in·sou·ci·ant • [in-SOO-see-ant] • \ in-ˈsü-sē-ənt \

- **adjective**

marked by blithe unconcern; nonchalant

Whereas I felt very nervous, Vicky was **insouciant** when we met the famous singer.

SYNONYMS

ANTONYMS

WRITING TIME!
Use *insouciant* in an original sentence of your own creation.

BONUS FUN TIME!
Express *insouciant* with a drawing or
invent a dictionary-style definition of your own.

orotund

or·o·tund • [OR-uh-tund] • \ ˈȯr-ə-ˌtənd \

- adjective
1. *loud, clear, and strong, as in tone or voice timbre*
2. *bombastic in speech or prose*

The president's **orotund** presentation made me want to follow her lead.

SYNONYMS

ANTONYMS

WRITING TIME!
Use *orotund* in an original sentence of your own creation.

BONUS FUN TIME!
Express *orotund* with a drawing or
invent a dictionary-style definition of your own.

perambulate

per·am·bu·late • [pe-RAM-byah-late] • \ pə-ˈram-byə-ˌlāt \

- verb

to walk through, about, or over; to stroll

We **perambulated** through the city all evening with no real destination in mind.

SYNONYMS

ANTONYMS

WRITING TIME!

Use *perambulate* in an original sentence of your own creation.

BONUS FUN TIME!

Express *perambulate* with a drawing or
invent a dictionary-style definition of your own.

perspicacious

per·spi·ca·cious • [pur-spi-KAY-shes] • \ ˌpər-spə-ˈkā-shəs \

- adjective

having keen judgment or understanding; acutely perceptive

Perspicacious detectives are the most successful.

SYNONYMS

ANTONYMS

WRITING TIME!
Use *perspicacious* in an original sentence of your own creation.

BONUS FUN TIME!
Express *perspicacious* with a drawing or
invent a dictionary-style definition of your own.

quidnunc

quid·nunc • [KWID-nungk] • \ ˈkwid-ˌnəŋk \

> **- noun**
>
> *a busybody; a nosy person*
>
> Our neighbor is such a **quidnunc**; she never minds her own business.

SYNONYMS

ANTONYMS

WRITING TIME!

Use *quidnunc* in an original sentence of your own creation.

BONUS FUN TIME!

Express *quidnunc* with a drawing or
invent a dictionary-style definition of your own.

redoubtable

re·doubt·a·ble • [rih-DOUT-uh-bull] • \ ri-ˈdau̇-tə-bəl \

- adjective

with personal qualities worthy of respect or fear

A **redoubtable** leader can inspire her followers to do almost anything.

SYNONYMS

ANTONYMS

WRITING TIME!

Use *redoubtable* in an original sentence of your own creation.

BONUS FUN TIME!

Express *redoubtable* with a drawing or
invent a dictionary-style definition of your own.

skulduggery

skul·dug·ge·ry • [skull-DUG-uh-ree] • \ ˌskəl-ˈdə-g(ə-)rē \

- noun

underhanded or unscrupulous behavior

Even for someone as dishonest as Jason, that **skulduggery** was surprising.

SYNONYMS

ANTONYMS

WRITING TIME!
Use *skulduggery* in an original sentence of your own creation.

BONUS FUN TIME!
Express *skulduggery* with a drawing or
invent a dictionary-style definition of your own.

somnolent

som·no·lent • [SOM-nuh-lent] • \ ˈsäm-nə-lənt \

> **- adjective**
>> 1. *sleepy; drowsy*
>> 2. *sleep-inducing*
>
> The **somnolent** lecturer droned on until the whole class fell asleep.

SYNONYMS

ANTONYMS

WRITING TIME!
Use *somnolent* in an original sentence of your own creation.

BONUS FUN TIME!
Express *somnolent* with a drawing or
invent a dictionary-style definition of your own.

toothsome

tooth·some • [TOOTH-sum] • \ ˈtüth-səm \

> **- adjective**
> *having a pleasing smell, taste, or appearance*
>
> There's something especially **toothsome** about a fresh bouquet of flowers.

SYNONYMS

ANTONYMS

WRITING TIME!
Use *toothsome* in an original sentence of your own creation.

BONUS FUN TIME!
Express *toothsome* with a drawing or
invent a dictionary-style definition of your own.

SECTION SIX: WORD REVIEW

Congratulations on learning fourteen more amazing words! Remember that the whole point of learning new vocabulary is to actually use it, so let's put your new vocabulary to use.

1. Review the words you've learned. Consider what comes to mind when you say the words themselves. How about when you read the definitions?

2. Circle at least **three** of your favorites. You'll get to use these in your very own story.

amanuensis — noun
1. somebody who takes dictation or copies manuscripts;
2. a writer's assistant

chimerical — adjective
1. wildly improbable or unrealistic
2. having a tendency to indulge in unrealistic fantasies

claque — noun
a group of people hired to applaud a performance

exculpate — verb
to free somebody from blame or accusation of guilt

flapdoodle — noun
foolish talk; nonsense

insouciant — adjective
marked by blithe unconcern; nonchalant

orotund — adjective
1. loud, clear, and strong, as in tone or voice timbre
2. bombastic in speech or prose

perambulate — verb
to walk through, about, or over; to stroll

perspicacious — adjective
having keen judgment or understanding; acutely perceptive

quidnunc — noun
a busybody; a nosy person

redoubtable — adjective
with personal qualities worthy of respect or fear

skulduggery — noun
underhanded or unscrupulous behavior

somnolent — adjective
1. sleepy; drowsy
2. sleep-inducing

toothsome — adjective
having a pleasing smell, taste, or appearance

STORY SIX

1. List the words you've chosen:

_____

2. Write a story that incorporates all of your chosen words. If you can't think of anything to write about, consider these suggestions:
   - Write a story that takes place entirely at your school.
   - Write a story in which you wake up and realize that you are an animal.

Title: _____

_____

_____

_____

_____

_____

_____

_____

_____

_____

INDEX OF WORDS USED

CPSIA information can be obtained
at www.ICGtesting.com
Printed in the USA
JSHW020000010521
14152JS00001B/5

9 781644 420492